Picture It!

Addy's Big Day

By **Stacy Pulley**, MS CCC-SLP

Illustrated by Ann G Rusky

thinking

I do a lot of fun things during the day.
At night, I want to tell Mommy and Daddy
about the good times I had.
I want to make sure I tell them everything!
But it is so hard to remember.

camera

So one day, Mommy showed me a real camera.

see it

When I looked, I could see
my best buddy Raffey in the camera.
I could see how the pictures
automatically popped up on the screen.

picture it

Mommy told me to take a 'picture' with mind
of the thing I wanted to talk about.
Then, I can see all the pictures in my mind,
like a camera, and use them to tell her
all about my day.

pancakes

This morning, I had pancakes for breakfast. I closed my eyes and I pictured them on my plate. I had three of them with bananas cut up on top. They looked like eyes. The syrup tasted sweet and it made my fingers sticky.

playing ball

Next, I went outside to play ball with Daddy.
The sun was so bright, when I pictured it,
I squinted my eyes. Daddy was smiling as he
pitched me the ball. I was trying so hard to
hit it without missing. I swung hard!

taking a nap

After baseball, I was tired.
I lay down for my nap in my warm bed
with my favorite green blanket.
I could hear the birds singing outside my
window. Raffey snuggled with me.
I could feel a breeze on my face.

fort

When I woke up from my nap, I built a fort with my brother, Lewis. Mommy let us use the sheets from her bed. They were white with blue flowers and felt soft and smooth. They smelled like fresh soap.The fort was as big as the couch. Lewis and I had so much fun!

popcorn

Later that night, we got hungry in the fort.
Daddy made us some microwave popcorn
for a snack. I saw the bag spinning in a circle.
I smelled butter and heard the pop!
Pop! Pop! When we opened the bag,
steam rushed out and felt hot on my hand!
The popcorn was yummy.

reading

At bedtime, I crawled under the covers of
Mommy and Daddy's bed. It was my favorite
time because it was just Mommy and me!
We read books together. We pointed to
the pictures and tried to guess what
the next page would say.

picture it

When I want to talk about my day,
I see the pictures in my mind just like the
pictures in the camera. I picture who I was
with, and what we were doing.
Then I focus on the details like sizes,
colors, smells, and sounds.

smile

Now, it is easy to tell Mommy and Daddy all
about my day when I see the pictures
in my mind. After I tell them everything
I pictured, they smile and say,
"Addy, you had a really big day!"

www.ingramcontent.com/pod-product-compliance
Lightning Source LLC
Chambersburg PA
CBHW040024050426

42452CB00002B/129